The Ginger Jar

Dedication

For my family.

The Ginger Jar

by

Shelly Ritthaler

Line art: Diana White
With appreciation to Gaydell Collier

First Edition
Raven Creek Press
Upton, Wyoming
1990

Library of Congress #90-91540
ISBN #09625745-1-1
Copyright ©1990 Shelly Ritthaler

Printed by Grelind Printing Center,
Rapid City, SD

❧ Contents ❧

The Ginger Jar

In 1987, the publisher of *The Black And White Magazine* telephoned me and wanted to know if I would be interested in writing a monthly column for them. I asked him what he had in mind, and he told me he wanted a humorous, spice-of-life sort of thing. *The Black And White* was a local advertising magazine distributed around the Black Hills of South Dakota and the northeastern corner of Wyoming. I said yes, I wanted to write for them.

After I agreed to do the column, it took me a long time to decide what to call it. Several titles came to mind. None of them satisfied me. One day, while dusting my bedroom, I reached to move the blue porcelain ginger jar on my dresser. The perfect title for the column struck me. I would to call it "The Ginger Jar."

Anciently, ginger jars were made in China out of a pure kaolin or China clay. After being fired, the result was a porcelain jar with a translucent quality. The jars, with their dome-shaped lids, were used to store preserved ginger, a tangy spice most commonly used in baking biscuits, cookies, gingerbread and pies. It can also be used to flavor meats, vegetables and for making tea or ginger ale. Ginger oil is used to make perfumes, and herbalists soak cloths or compresses in a ginger tea solution and use them for easing pain. In China, the underground stems of the ginger plant are peeled and boiled in a syrup to preserve them. Traditionally, the preserved ginger was stored in covered, globular jars which came to be known as ginger jars.

It is believed the ginger jars had another special use. During the Chinese New Year celebration the jar was filled with candy, ginger, tea or other treats and given as a gift. The contents of the jar were kept by the recipient. The jar was then returned to the giver.

In a sense, the title was appropriate for the magazine column. It came to be like a ginger jar which I filled with some of the stories and thoughts that have eased my pains and given aroma and spice to my life. I have gathered those old columns together, added some new ones and put them together for this book. In this collection, there are stories about my husband, Reuben, a six-foot-tall cowboy with eyes the color of a Wyoming summer sky. There is Reuben's sister, Kenda. She had just started high school when her father, a widower, remarried and moved from the ranch to town. Kenda missed the place where she had grown up and came back to live with us and share our home and our lives. We adopted Min Dee when she was two years old. Over the years, this skinny little girl with her red-brown hair and easygoing smile has taught me much about life and inspired me in many ways.

I hope that you, the reader, will enjoy the gift of these stories. ✺

Bad Habits

I am a perfectionist. I have no bad habits. On New Year's Day each year my husband, Reuben, and I sit down together and plan our new year's resolutions. I usually resolve to be a better wife and mother. Reuben always promises to give up chewing tobacco.

When we sat down last year, Reuben said, "This time I'm really going to do it. I am going to give up chewing."

I said, "I'll go for being a better wife and mother."

"That's not fair," he accused. "You never try to give up any bad habits."

"Bad habits?" I blinked a couple of times. "Bad habits? Why, Sweetheart," I said gently, "you know I don't have any bad habits."

"Oh, yeah?" he countered. "What do you call this?" He took a bowl of junior-size candy bars from the cupboard and spilled them onto the table.

"I call it a few candy bars."

"What about this?" He yanked open the freezer door of the refrigerator and started to rummage. After he pulled out three more sacks of junior-size candy bars and two eight-ounce chocolate bars, he snorted, "And what do you call this?"

I looked at the ceiling and nonchalantly said, "Oh, um, just a few more candy bars."

"Ha, you think I don't know about this?" he taunted as he headed for the freezer in the garage. "I saw what you had hidden in here the last time you asked me to get out a package of hamburger."

I followed him to the garage. He threw open the freezer lid and proceeded to unload two dozen full-size Milky Way bars, a half dozen Snickers, one dozen Hershey's plain (and two more with-almonds) chocolate bars, three dozen assorted packages of M&M's plain and peanut candies and two boxes of Girl Scout Thin Mint cookies. "Mighty gosh, woman, isn't this a bit much?"

"Well," I snapped, "you never know when you might get hungry for a little chocolate."

"A little chocolate? A little chocolate? I'd give a hundred-to-one odds that you have more stashed somewhere else."

I tossed my candy bars back into the freezer and chased him into the house.

"What about your office?" he demanded.

Before I could answer, he had the file cabinet drawers open. "What do we have here? Two sacks of chocolate kisses, a half sack of chocolate-covered peanuts and a box of chocolate-covered caramels. Oh, excuse me, the caramel box is empty." He threw it at me. "Where else? Come on, come clean. Fess up."

"You're being mean," I pouted.

"Mean?" He laughed. "I'll give a thousand-to-one odds you have more packed away."

Before I could protest, he headed for our bedroom. From out of my nightstand drawer, he pulled a package of chocolate-covered malted balls and what was left of a box of chocolate turtles. "Is that it?" he asked.

4

"You got me dead to right." I faked a laugh. "That must be it." Consciously, I tried not to look, but subconsciously, my brains let my gaze wander over toward the dresser.

"Aha," he shouted as he yanked out the top drawer and dumped its contents on the bed.

There, among my unmentionable clothing, was the good stuff—Swiss chocolate with hazelnut and raspberry fillings, French chocolate mints and chocolate truffles.

Reuben looked at me in exasperated disbelief. "This," he said with a slight hiss, "is an obsession."

"See," I pointed out triumphantly, "I told you I don't have any bad habits." ✄

The Common Cold

They call it the common cold. The symptoms vary in their degree of severity but usually include coughing, sneezing, wheezing, runny nose, watery eyes, aching muscles, fever and congestion. Although medical science says there is no proven cure, it hasn't stopped some of the more inventive people I have known from devising their own methods of medicinal magic when it comes to the common cold.

I always keep a supply of over-the-counter cold remedies on hand. But I get the most relief and comfort for my colds by wrapping up in a quilt and sipping a cup of herbal tea with a slice of lemon and a teaspoon of honey in it.

My grandmother used to make a potion out of sliced onions and molasses. Just trying to imagine the taste of it gives me the shudders. My mother remembers admitting to having very few, if any, colds when she was a child. I think the operative word here is "admitting." If Mom sneezed or coughed, she probably did it behind the barn out of my grandmother's range of hearing.

Reuben's grandmother, Emma, was a real proponent of greasing. She believed that there isn't any illness that can't benefit from a good rubdown with Ben Gay, especially the big "C" diseases—coughs, colds, cramps, cancer. If Gramma Emma noticed that you were sniffling or sneezing, she'd squint one eye, shake an ominous finger at you and say, "You be sure to grease."

The weirdest cure I've ever heard is to spray your chest with WD-40. Yes, the same WD-40 lubricating spray used to unstick sticky closet doors and loosen tight hinges. The bizarre thing is, the idea has a logical basis. If it can loosen up your closet doors and hinges, it should loosen up your congested chest as well. I can't personally recommend it. I've never had the guts to try it, but the person who told me about it swears it works like a charm.

One time we had a friend visiting us. While here, he caught a terrible cold. That night, just before bedtime, I opened up my medicinal arsenal for him. I offered cough syrups, nighttime remedies, daytime relievers, cold pills, decongestants, throat lozenges, Ben Gay, Vicks, herbal tea and honey. I even showed him my can of WD-40 and explained its use.

He blinked his red, watery eyes, wiped his nose, grabbed the bottle of aspirin and said, "Thanks, Doc, but I think I'll take a couple of these, get a good night's sleep and check with you in the morning."

The next day, when he came downstairs for breakfast, all of his cold symptoms were gone.

"You mean to tell me your cold is cured?" I asked. "In one night? Must have been an uncommon cold. That or you tried the WD-40."

He laughed at me. "No, Doc, I swear, I took two aspirins, fell right to sleep and checked with my favorite doctor this morning."

I've been giving it a lot of thought. Take two aspirins and call the doctor in the morning? As far as cures go, I wonder if there's something to it? &

The
Last Heartache

When I got married, I was naive enough to believe I would never have to suffer another heartache. I was certain a happy marriage would protect me from ever having my heart ripped out and stomped on again.

I was painfully wrong. One day, Min Dee came home from kindergarten with a long, miserable face. She sighed as I fixed her a snack. "What's wrong, Gloomy-Gus?" I asked.

A tear slipped down her cheek. "I told David that I love him."

"And what did he say?" I pulled her into my lap and hugged her.

"He said he doesn't love me because he loves Kati."

"I'm sorry, Sweetheart, but sometimes things work out that way. Does it help to know that I love you?"

"No," she sobbed as she drooped her head over my shoulder. "I wanted to marry David."

My chest was tearing open. How could that little, playground twerp break my daughter's heart? I remembered the first time I fell in love. I was in first grade; he was in third. His name was Russell, and he had blonde hair, blue eyes and his own football. This was the only boy I would ever love in my whole life. Then one day I saw him kiss my best friend, Judy. They were on the lunchroom steps. I was so devastated I couldn't look at another boy until I was in the sixth grade. I squeezed Min Dee. "Honest, it won't hurt forever," I told her. "What do you say we drown our sorrows in a root beer float?"

A week later, Min Dee came home from school with a glowing smile on her face. "Guess what, Mom? I told Greg that I love him."

I bit my cheek to keep from smiling. "You did? What did he say?"

"He didn't say anything. He just put his hands in his pockets and smiled."

If that isn't a sign of true love, I've never seen one. But what about next week? Next year? Do these fellows realize that if they break her heart, they'll be breaking mine as well? I know I will hurt for her as much as she hurts for herself. Probably more.

I thought I had suffered my last heartache. What a laugh. This is only the beginning. How am I going to survive her pain when a certain boy doesn't ask her to dance at her first junior high school dance? What about the jerk who stands her up, or the creep who asks someone else to prom and everything else in between?

It's clear—each of Min Dee's heartaches will be my own. And when her wedding day comes, I'm certain I will entertain thoughts of having suffered my last heartache. And I'll live in the bliss of that illusion until, heaven help me, my grandchildren discover love. ❧

Hound Dog Eyes

When Min Dee was four years old, she went through her "why" stage. She wanted to know everything. Why do birds fly? Why does the sun shine in the day and the moon at night? Why do I have to eat potatoes? Why can't I drive the car? Why can't I have my ears pierced?

She tested my powers of explanation on more than one occasion. I always tried to give wonderful, inspired and carefully-worded answers. She'd listen, look at me and respond to my answer with an even more demanding, "Why?"

One day, while sitting at the table smearing her mashed potatoes around her plate to make it look like she had eaten some of them, she asked, "Mom? Why did you marry Daddy?"

Without thinking, I answered, "Because I loved him."

"Why?"

"Because I wanted to be with him all the time."

"Why?"

"Because there was something about him I couldn't resist."

"Why?"

"Well. . . ." By now she had my full attention, or at least the question did. "Well. . . ." I tried to change the subject. "Min Dee, eat your potatoes."

"Why?"

In order to escape her questions, I told her she didn't have to clean her plate and excused her from the table. She flashed out of her chair and disappeared before I had a chance to change my mind. The question floated in and out of my subconscious for a long time. Why DID I marry Reuben? To be honest, I couldn't come up with a good, concrete answer. After all, how do you put into words or describe the thing that makes you love another person? Philosophical, clinical and psychological explanations leave you with a dissatisfied sense or feeling that they really don't have the answers either.

I came as close as I think I'll ever get to an answer when I met Bailey. Bailey is a beagle. He is the most obnoxious, bone-headed, stubborn, noisy dog in three counties. He belongs to me.

When I got him, he was in double deep trouble and within minutes of breathing his last breath. At that time he belonged to a friend of mine. Bailey had been given to his daughter by one of her boyfriends. When the daughter went to college, Bailey became his. It would have been fine, if it hadn't been for Bailey's breeding. His breeding is what got him into trouble. He is a registered, pedigreed dog. Given his upper-crust breeding, it's only natural that his appetite could never be satisfied with ordinary, everyday, run-of-the-mill, store-bought, dry dog food. No. Bailey craved a more patrician diet and started to eat my friend's wife's peacocks. These weren't your ordinary, everyday, run-of-the-mill, store-bought peacocks either. These peacocks were the direct descendants of a set of peacocks that were brought to the west, their cages carefully secured in a spot in the back of a covered wagon, when her ancestors came to this county to homestead in the early 1900s.

At first, Bailey only ate a peachick now and then. My friend's family blamed the missing birds on the foxes. He slipped up on a peahen or two. The coyotes took a fall for the diminished herd of birds. Then the little mutt went for one of the male peacocks. He was discovered, snout deep, in an elegant pile of blue and emerald plumage. By then, he was beyond forgiveness. For Bailey, the end was at hand. About that time, I drove into their yard. They asked me if I was interested in saving a two-bit dog's life.

I looked down. Bailey crouched by the pickup tire and looked up at me. He thumped his tail and flopped his tongue out of a smiling, open mouth. But the thing that got to me was his hound dog eyes. I'll never forget looking into those sparkley wet eyes that seemed to beg, "Please, take me home, take care of me, love me. Love me. Love me."

I should have said no. For some reason, I couldn't resist those eyes. We don't have peacocks, and I had given up raising chickens; Bailey would be safe. I told him he would have to learn to survive on a subsistence diet of Co-op dog food and table scraps. I opened the pickup door and slapped my leg. Without hesitating, he jumped up and made himself comfy in the middle of the seat.

When we got home, Bailey's arrival was quite an occasion. Our ranch neighborhood recognizes and acknowledges only two breeds of dogs—young cow dogs and old cow dogs. The hired men teased me, kidded me, and called my dog Beetle Bailey. They all had a good laugh until the next morning. That's when we knew, without a doubt, that Bailey's favorite thing, even more than eating peacocks, is baying at the moon. Can that little mongrel howl! We're not talking about one or two barks. No, we are talking about a siren song that starts as a low, quivering moan, then rises into a higher and higher-pitched, gut-sucking vibrato wail.

I tried to discipline him, but every time I shook my finger and screamed at him, he gave me the look, that—you love me, you need me, you can't resist me—look. We all finally ended up learning to sleep through Bailey's unique rendition of a moonlight sonata.

Whenever Bailey does something bad, I try to yell at him. But I get "the look." One day, I had been to the grocery store. I was packing the first load of groceries into the house and had left the car door open. By the time I returned, Bailey was standing on the seat finishing off the second of two packages of cookies. I screamed, "BAILEY!" He rolled over on his back. From his upside-down vantage point on the seat, he gave me "the look" and had me right where he wanted me.

Over time, with much trial and tribulation, we have grown used to Bailey and his personality. During that same time, Min Dee outgrew her "why?" stage and has started asking more complex questions. She has also learned to persist in asking a question until she gets a full and satisfying answer. One night, as I was tucking her into bed, she asked me if I thought she would ever get married. I kissed her nose and told her she would if it was what she wanted. She asked, "Did Daddy ask you to marry him?" I nodded. "Did you say yes?" I nodded again. "How come?"

I took a deep breath and tried to tell her I didn't know exactly, specifically why. There was something about the way he asked me. Something about the way he looked. Something in the look in his eyes. That's when I knew the answer. I gave her a hug, smiled and said, "I married Daddy because I'm a sucker for hound dog eyes."

She looked at me, shook her head, snuggled into her quilt and mumbled, "Mom, you're weird."

I'll give her a few more years. Someday, I'm sure, she's going to want me to explain love and romance. And then I'll tell her everything I know about those hound dog eyes. ❧

Motivation

It's easy to get busy with or so involved in other activities that it's hard to get motivated to do some of life's less desirable tasks like cleaning the house, balancing your checkbook and paying the bills.

One of the few things I love better than chocolate is my computer. I can spend hours and days in front of it. As I sit there, I imagine I am the world's greatest author. The words appearing on the screen are going to become the next, critically-acclaimed, best-selling, great American novel. It's easy—too easy—to spend all my time in front of my computer screen rather than doing other mundane, boring sorts of things.

One day, in the middle of March, I told myself, "I should take time to clean the house, balance my checkbook and pay the bills." But I just couldn't seem to get motivated to do it. At the end of the month, the power company sent me a letter that said, "Dear Valued Customer, Did you forget to send your payment? Please send remittance today." I distinctly remember telling myself as I sat down at my computer, "I should pay the bills." But once I sat down, I became the next soon-to-be-famous writer and promptly forgot about the bills.

At the end of April, the power company sent me a note. "Your bill is overdue, please send payment immediately. Failure to pay could mean a disconnection of your services. We value you as a customer. Please send payment NOW."

A friend of mine told me I would be able to motivate myself if I made a list of the things I needed to get done. Before I allowed myself to sit in front of the computer, I must first complete the task at the top of the list. It seemed like a good idea to me. Perhaps a reward system was what I needed to help me get motivated.

I made a list. Balance the checkbook, pay bills, and clean the house were the top three items on the page. I added a few other jobs I had neglected for a long time and was well on my way to being motivated. Then I lost the list. When I tried to find it and couldn't, I told myself, "I should have put 'clean the house' in the number one spot on the list." Rather than waste valuable time in a futile search, I went to work at my computer in order to give myself a little more time to remember where I put the list.

As the end of May rolled around, I got a rather short note from the power company. It said, in red ink, "If you don't pay your bill or contact us by tomorrow, your service will be disconnected. You will no longer be a valued customer." At that moment, I realized that when I ceased to be a valued customer, I would no longer have electricity. You can't run a computer without electricity. I broke into a cold sweat and shivered; my mouth went dry.

If the people at the power company ever decide to branch out and diversify their operations, I think they could make a fortune giving lessons in motivation. I did not wait to balance my checkbook and clean my house. I did not walk,

I did not run, I drove my car, very fast, right up to the front door of the power company business office. I wrote a check and paid my bill—IN FULL.

Once I had written the check, I had to balance the checkbook so I wouldn't overdraft it. Since I had the checkbook balanced, I decided it was a good time to get the other bills paid. In order to do that, I had to clean the house to make sure I had all of them gathered together.

At the end of June, when I paid my electric bill, I enclosed a short note just to let the good people at the power company know how much I appreciate being one of their valued, motivated customers. ✒

Without Wings

When Min Dee was four years old, our hired ranch hand found two large eagle feathers lying on the ground in one of our pastures. He gave them to Min Dee and said, "Now you have a set of wings."

Teasing, Reuben added, "If you hold one in each hand and flap them hard enough, you'll be able to fly." Min Dee believed him and spent most of the rest of that summer racing back and forth across the yard, madly flapping the feathers, trying her best to fly.

When winter came the feathers were put into a vase on her dresser. I thought she forgot about them until the next summer. Once again, she was running back and forth across the yard trying to fly. By the end of July, she got discouraged and told Reuben, "Dad, I flap and flap and flap as hard as I can, but I still can't fly."

Not willing to let go of the joke, Reuben said, "Maybe there hasn't been enough wind to get you picked up off the ground. Once you get off the ground, you'll be flying."

That afternoon I caught her on top of the dog house, feathers outstretched, poised for flight. "Min Dee, you get down from there before you break your neck," I yelled.

"But Mom," she howled. "How can I fly if I don't get off the ground?"

I stopped then and there and tried to explain the physics of aviation. I told her she needed more than a couple of feathers to fly. Her disappointment showed in the tears that welled up in her eyes. I tried to make her feel better by telling her that when she got older, she could take lessons and learn to fly a real airplane. She turned away saying, "I wanted to fly all by myself."

The feather wings went back into the vase and were finally forgotten after Min Dee started kindergarten that fall. When I took her to school for her first day, we got out of the car and stood on the sidewalk. She said, "Mom, you don't need to walk with me, I'm big now."

"I know you're big," I said trying not to cry. "I just wanted to see how nice your new classroom looks. If that's okay?"

She didn't answer, and we quietly walked toward the big double door. Halfway to the building, she reached up and took my hand. "Mom? Do you need me to hold on to you?"

"I sure do." I took her hand, smiled and exercised every ounce of self-control I possessed to keep from grabbing her, throwing her back into the car, and taking her home with me.

I survived that day and the school days that followed as she began to grow academically and socially. Toward the end of the school year, I was reminded of Min Dee's first day of school and the eagle feather wings when she was invited to a birthday party. On the day of the party, I drove her to her classmate's house and parked next to the curb. Turning off the key, I started to get out of the car. Min Dee looked at me and said, "Mom, you don't need to go. I know how to ring the doorbell."

"Oh, um—well, I was just going to help you a little." I jumped out, ran around the car and opened her door. "Are you sure you don't want me to walk you up the sidewalk?" I asked.

"I'm sure."

"Want me to carry the present for you?" I was starting to feel like a tag-along sibling.

"I can get it."

"What if you can't reach the doorbell?"

"Mom," she groaned, rolling her eyes, "I can always knock."

By then, the other little girls poured out of the house. Min Dee ran to join them. They huddled together and giggled on the porch for a few seconds before they turned, went into the house and closed the door. I stood alone on the curb next to the car and felt sorry for myself. It's hard to accept that she doesn't need me to hold her hand and walk with her, that her world quickly grows apart from mine. I don't have to wait for her to grow up and take flying lessons to replace the eagle feathers. She doesn't need an airplane to fly away. She already flies—without wings. ❧

Keeper of
the Fish

Reuben's mother passed away two years after he and I were married. A year later, his father remarried, retired from ranching and moved to town. Reuben and I took over the operation of the ranch and moved from the bunkhouse into the main ranch house. When we moved, I inherited Reuben's mother's freezer. Some of the food inside of it was outdated. I went to work cleaning it out. I put all of the old vegetables and fruits into a large bucket so I could give them to the chickens to eat.

When I got to the bottom of the freezer, I found an aluminum foil-wrapped package. I unwound the foil and ended up holding an ancient-looking fish. It had been in the freezer so long, it was freeze dried. "Oh gross," I said as I dropped it like a hot potato on top of the refuse in the almost-filled bucket. I decided to take a break and lugged the bucket down to the chicken pen and dumped it. Chickens flocked from all corners of the barnyard to get a share of the unexpected treat. One brave rooster pecked at the old fish, shook his head, then dropped a little chip of dried meat he had taken from the side of the fish. I told the rooster, "My sentiments exactly."

I went back to the house and was wiping out the empty freezer when Reuben came home. He stepped into the garage and asked me what I was doing. "I'm getting this freezer cleaned out. There was quite a bit of old stuff in here. You wouldn't believe the fish I found."

"The fish!" His eyes were wide with panic. He gasped in a horror-stricken voice, "What did you do with the fish?"

"I gave it to the chickens. The thing was all dried out. It wasn't any good," I told him.

"You threw away the fish?" His voice was accusing, and he gave me a distant, evil look. "You threw away Dad's fish?"

Before I could answer, he ran out of the garage and down to the chicken house. As I watched him pick up the fish and gently carry it back to the house, I got the distinct feeling my husband had lost his marbles. That, or I was missing some vital piece of information which would explain his weird behavior.

Reuben stepped into the garage and reverently held the fish toward me. "A chicken tried to eat him, but I got there in time." He pointed to the small hole I had seen the rooster peck. "Other than that he's fine. Do you have some foil?" he asked. "I need to get him wrapped up again."

"Reuben," I told him gently, "the fish is no good."

He looked wounded and said, "You don't understand. This is Dad's fish." He then explained how his mom and dad had gone on a fishing trip not long after they were married. It was the first time his dad had ever been fishing. On that trip, he caught the fish. Reuben's mother had been so proud of it, she wanted to have it mounted. They brought it home, wrapped it and put it in the freezer until they could take it to a taxidermist. But time slipped away. The fish never made it to the taxidermist. Instead, it had spent almost forty years in the bottom of the freezer.

26

"If you have some foil," Reuben said, "I want to put him back in the freezer right away." My first inclination was to laugh at the idea of keeping a forty-year-old fish in my freezer. This had to be the limit of sentimentality. But Reuben was sincere. Without a word, I went into the house for the aluminum foil. When I returned, I took the fish from him and carefully wrapped it in two layers of silver before handing it back to him. "I'm sorry," I said as he laid the fish in the freezer. "I didn't know what it meant to you and your family."

At the time, I honestly didn't understand. When I was a child, my family moved almost every year. We didn't keep or accumulate things. We got rid of everything that wasn't worth packing and unpacking. When I met Reuben, one of the things that attracted me to him was the permanence and stability of belonging to a family that had lived in one place for three generations. His grandparents had homesteaded the ranch, his father purchased it from them, and Reuben planned to step into his father's place and buy the ranch from him. Because they stayed in one place, they could keep traditions, a lifestyle, their occupation and things, like a dried-out fish, to pass on to the next generation.

That old fish meant more to me later that summer when I learned to farm. Reuben sat me on a tractor with a cultivator hooked to the back. He told me how to keep the cultivator lined up so I could work in even rows. He showed me how to turn the tractor so that I wouldn't run the tractor tires over the top of the cultivator. He explained that I was going to summer fallow. In the spring, after the snow on the fields has melted into the ground and it dries, the soil is hardened and must be broken up and loosened with the curved metal teeth on a cultivator. This kills the weeds and tears open the ground so that it can absorb rainwater. It prepares the soil for planting and is called summer fallowing.

When I got the hang of driving the tractor, Reuben let me farm by myself. As I worked my way around the field, I remembered Reuben telling me that at one time, this field was sage-covered prairie land. His grandfather had selected this piece of land, had turned the sod and plowed it for the first time. His father had farmed it, and even expanded the field. I turned and looked over my shoulder and watched the dirt turn up and over itself as the cultivator ripped through it.

I thought about the winter wheat we wanted to plant later. After we planted the wheat seed in the fall, it would lie in the ground over the winter. In the spring, it would sprout and grow. When autumn came again, and the heads turned gold, we would combine and sell the grain to the elevator. Eventually it would be made into flour, most of which would be sold to a baking company to make bread. Thinking about all of this brought to mind the biblical story of the loaves and the fishes. In the story, a multitude of people were fed with five loaves of bread and two fishes. For the first time, I fully realized what I had married into, become a part of and an heir to.

I am following an age-old occupation started by people who gave up a life of roving and hunting so they could settle in one place, gather their families around them and cultivate fields to plant wheat to make bread for themselves, their families and multitudes of people. By pulling a cultivator in continuous circles around a field, I have become an intimate part of that tradition. My work will be added to the work of those who have come and gone before me. I am a part of a way of life that has the luxury of growing in one place, of being able to keep things like an age-old lifestyle and a forty-year-old fish.

A while back, Reuben, Min Dee and I were rearranging the freezer to make room for a beef we were having butchered. Reuben pulled the fish out of the bottom corner, unwrapped it and showed it to Min Dee. He told her the story of how his dad caught the fish. Then he turned it over. "And see here," he said as he pointed to the little pecked-out hole. "This is where Mommy tried to feed him to the chickens."

And now, it all fits together—the pieces of becoming a part of an agricultural way of life, of being a part of the chain and keeping it to pass down. It's the same as having my part of the story added to the story of the forty-year-old fish in my freezer. ✄

The Gofer

After my father-in-law retired from ranching and moved to town, I became the new gofer. (As in go-fer this, go-fer that.) I have decided it is a job designed to drive women crazy.

It would seem like a simple thing to drive to town, pick up a few things and bring them home. I found out that being a gofer can involve more problems than a cat can have kittens.

The biggest problem is the tremendous amount of driving. The closest, large town I can get supplies and parts at is a 96-mile round-trip. Once I get there, the businesses are either out of, have to order, or don't have exactly what I need. Or worse, they need to know some minute, obscure bit of information which I have no way of knowing.

Take for example, the day Reuben sent me for some four-inch wooden fence posts. This meant a trip to Belle Fourche, South Dakota, a 180-mile drive there and back. When I arrived, the salesman at the Cenex told me, "Sorry, I just ran out of fours; a guy just bought the last of what I had. I can

31

order some for you. Takes a week and a half." I shook my head. "I have threes and sixes," he added. "Would they work?" He handed me the phone. "Wanna call your husband and ask?"

"No, thank you," I said, trying to be polite as I thought, "If my husband had time to sit around the kitchen and answer the telephone, he would be here now."

Then there was the time I went after a five-gallon can of number three motor oil. The kid behind the counter at the Co-op said, "Sorry, we don't get number three oil any more. We got Idol oil thirty two, thirty three, and thirty five."

"Which is the same as number three?" I asked. He shrugged. Before long, I had two mechanics, the bookkeeper and the manager leaning over a can of number 33, arguing. I finally got impatient. "Tell you what," I said, "let's take a vote." The mechanics and the manager voted for 33, the book-keeper abstained, and the kid behind the counter voted for 35.

As I paid for a can of 33, I asked him why he voted for the 35. He told me he thought the 33 was a little thin, but that it would probably be all right. "What does a pimple-faced, punk kid know anyway?" I told myself as I drove home with my can of 33.

That night I asked Reuben if the oil was okay. He said, "It's a little thin, but it'll work."

I would like an answer to one question: why is it I always manage to find the salesman or mechanic who knows as much or a little less than I do? When you consider the fact that I am totally and completely mechanically inept, it's pretty bad. I do well to run my electric can opener. It took me three years to figure out what all the buttons on my microwave oven are for.

One day I went to town to get some bushings for the pickup. The parts man brought out two odd-looking things and said, "Is this what you need?"

I said, "You're asking me? Mister, I don't know a bushing from a ball bearing." He laughed and put them into a sack. I got into my car and began my usual incantation, "Please let this be the right stuff. Please let this be the right stuff."

When I arrived home, I asked Reuben if they were the right parts and held my breath. He looked into the sack. "Yep, they're the right ones. But there's only two here. There should be three." I got back in the car. The radio was blasting, "On The Road Again." I hate that song.

These things happen all the time. Usually I take it all in stride, try to maintain my sense of humor and, most importantly, my sanity. But one day, I lost it completely. My parents were coming to visit, which they don't do often enough. Reuben came into the house with a worried look on his face and said, "The hay feeder broke down. I smashed a couple of master links. They hold the chains on the feeder bed together. I can't feed until I fix it."

I had spent two days planning a special, family dinner and was just slipping a homemade angel food cake into the oven. "I'm sorry," he said as I stepped away from the stove. "I know your folks are on their way. I'd go myself, but it'll take me two hours to tear the feeder down. I can do that while you're gone; then I'll be ready for the links by the time you get back."

I swallowed a lump in my throat, turned off the oven and hoped the cake would go ahead and finish baking. "You could pick up some chicken at the drive-in," he added in an apologetic voice.

The unexpected trip ruined everything. By the time I walked into the parts store, I felt pretty low. I asked the salesman for three master links. He laid three, tiny, silver gizmos in the palm of my hand. Each was about the size of a penny. "That'll be a dollar fifty-six," he chirped.

"A dollar fifty-six?" Something snapped. I couldn't help myself. "Do you mean to tell me that I have five hundred hungry cows that haven't been fed because of a part that costs fifty cents? Are you telling me I drove all this way for parts that cost a dollar fifty-six?" My voice rose to a fevered pitch. "A dollar fifty-six? Do you know my angel food cake is as flat as a pancake, my kitchen sink is full of dirty dishes, and my mom and dad have to eat bucket chicken for lunch?" I slapped two dollars on the counter and screeched, "There! Keep the change!"

As I stormed out the door, I heard him mutter, "Women. I will never understand women." ❧

My Name
Isn't Someone

"Someone needs to run to town right away this afternoon."

I shook the soapy dishwater from my hands and turned around to face Reuben. He was leaning in the doorway between the kitchen and porch. His coveralls looked like a modern art creation done in multiple colors of mud, grease and manure. Peeking out from under the brim of his misshapen hat, he watched for my reaction.

"Someone needs to go sign a note to cover the check I wrote for that extra feed last week," he said. "The check will probably be back today." He gave me his "I'm-a-bad-boy-but-I-know-you'll-forgive-me" smile. "Sorry, I sorta forgot to tell you about it," he added.

Before I could start ranting and raving, he planted one muddy overboot in the middle of the kitchen floor, leaned in toward me, slapped me on the behind, and dashed out the door shouting, "You're a pal, I'll love you forever."

I would have gone to the door and chastised him for forgetting to tell me about the check and for the mud on the floor, but the hands on the clock allowed him to escape. It was 2:30 p.m. The bank closes at 3:00. It takes exactly 30 minutes to travel to town on our dirt roads—20 minutes if you drive like Mario Andretti. "If the roads aren't too muddy, I can make it," I thought.

Grabbing my purse, deposit slips and coat, I jumped into the car. Halfway to town, I realized I was wearing my jeans with the hole in the patch on the left knee, my worst tennis shoes and my favorite old sweatshirt whose most attractive features include a 1776-1976 Bicentennial logo, a few small holes and a generous spattering of green sheep paint.

My reflection in the rearview mirror made me wonder whether I had combed my hair that morning or not. Fortunately, I slipped into the bank and took care of my business just as they were starting to lock the door.

Normally, driving home from town is one of my greatest pleasures. On that day, the sun was shining with a promise of warmer spring days to come. A handful of frisky calves frolicked on one of the hillsides. In the pastures, impish lambs chased each other around while their mothers nibbled on young shoots of greening grass. All of this should have made me feel contented. But irritation overwhelmed and squelched my satisfaction.

No, it wasn't the flying trip to town that bothered me—it was that "someone" business.

I do have a name. It's listed on my birth certificate, driver's license and credit cards. I'm surprised Reuben failed to notice. It's spelled out on our marriage certificate.

I don't know when it started. Calling out for "someone" has always been Reuben's method of asking me to do something. "Can someone take me to my tractor?" "Can someone drive the pickup for me?" "I'm stuck; can someone give me a pull?" "Did someone make a pot of coffee?"

I was tired of it and decided things are going to change. My name isn't Someone! I was going to go home and insist that I be called by my given name. What's more, I was going to let it be known that I wouldn't mind if a "please" were thrown in now and then as well.

While fixing supper that night, I prepared to present my case. Reuben came in the back door, and my good intentions faded when I heard the familiar, but unexpected, voice of Jim, our neighbor, coming from behind my husband. "Hi, make the bank?" Reuben asked. I nodded and tried not to show my disappointment. I knew I wouldn't be able to talk to him during dinner. "Jim's been helping me with a calf this afternoon," Reuben told me. "S'pose we could have a bite of supper before he heads home?"

As we sat down to eat, Reuben said, "By the way, there's a bum calf down in the barn. Someone's going to have to feed him before too long." My teeth grated together.

Right after supper, Jim got ready to leave. I walked him to the porch, waited for him to put on his coveralls, overboots, and hat, then told him goodbye and shut the door behind him. Now was my chance.

I dashed through the kitchen and around the corner into the living room. Too late! Reuben was already asleep in the recliner. I picked up an afghan, shook it out and laid it over him. He didn't even stir when I kissed him softly on the cheek.

While I mixed the powdered milk replacer with warm water for the calf, I made a resolution. I would take a stand on this issue right after we were done calving. That made me feel a little better. I put on my old down-filled coat, stuffed my hair into a stocking cap, and stepped outside to find that the balmy spring day had turned into a blustery, near-winter night. Luckily, the milk in the bottle gave enough heat to warm my fingers.

Later, on the way back to the house, I remembered that right after calving comes farming, then branding, then haying, summer fallowing, weaning, shipping, winter feeding, then—sigh—calving again.

My milky, wet fingers shivered in the cold air. The empty bottle offered no warmth. I dug into my coat pockets. Nothing.

"On a cold night like this," I thought, "how could someone forget her mittens?" ❧

Steamy Romance

I spent two years of my life working as the editor and historian for a local history book. During that time, little else occupied my mind. When I was finishing the project and getting it ready to go to the publisher, I looked at the manuscript pages piled on my desk. For the first time in two years, the idea of doing something new occurred to me.

Leaving my office, I wandered out to the living room where Reuben was reading the paper and watching the late news. "I was thinking," I said, "about what I'm going to do now that I'm done with the history book."

He briefly looked over the top of the paper and said, "Oh?"

"What do you think if I try something totally different, something exciting, something fun, something that doesn't require research or a lot of thought? I need to cool off my brains."

A monotone, "Oh?" came from behind the paper.

"What would you think if I wrote a steamy romance novel?"

"Oh?"

"But then, again, that might require some research after all."

"Oh?"

"Yeah, like for the sake and purpose of research, you could surprise me with a dozen roses, or a box of French chocolate mints, or some frilly article of intimate apparel."

"Oh?"

"Or maybe, we could get outrageous and go to Hawaii for a week. I could do a lot of steamy romance research while we're there. If the research goes well, we could, maybe, stay for two weeks."

"Oh?" This time he looked over his paper. "I thought you were tired of research. Why don't you write a steamy, western romance? You spent all that time studying cowboys and Indians." He disappeared behind the paper again.

"Well sure, I studied cowboys and Indians, but that's not where I'm lacking the expertise. I was thinking about the romance end of things. That's where I need to concentrate my energy and efforts. Hawaii would be the ideal place to do some heavy-duty research. With palm trees blowing in soft breezes; warm, sandy beaches; and flowers, all those gorgeous flowers; the ocean air; me in a brand new bikini. It's the perfect setting for a romantic adventure story. I'd want my descriptions to be accurate, and there's nothing like firsthand experience and the benefits that come from on-the-spot research. Don't you think, Reuben? Reuben, don't you think? Reuben?"

I peeked over the paper. He was sound asleep. "Now there's a man with nothing on his mind," I whispered as I took the paper out of his hands and folded it. Turning off the TV, I went back to my office.

"Then again," I said to myself as I sat in front of the keyboard, "someone really should write a history of the petroleum industry. That could be fun. Or, for excitement, I might study medieval religious customs. Or, wow, I could get wild and crazy and look into the lifestyles and daily habits of Peruvian monks. . . ." 🐾

Graders Camp

I studied history in high school and college, but it wasn't until I researched and wrote a history book on my own, that history really meant something to me. Before, it was all facts and dates. Now, I can't look at the past or the future in the same way.

The book I wrote covered the history of Weston County, Wyoming. It started with the dinosaurs and came forward to the 1980s. The manuscript ended up being about 300 pages long. In all of that information, one story still stands out in my mind. I think about it over and over again. It is the story of a railroad graders camp.

In 1889, the Burlington Northern Railroad Company extended its northern rail lines from Edgemont, South Dakota, into northeastern Wyoming. Wherever the railroad went, commerce and industry followed, as there was money to be made catering to the construction crews and camps of workers that followed the lines.

Before the steel tracks could be laid, the rail beds had to be graded and built using horse-drawn fresnos and slips. The grading crews that did this work lived in camps that followed the progress of the construction. The camps were made up of graders, construction workers, their families and a cook or two. A camp like this followed the railroad building through northeastern Wyoming. The route crossed the old Cheyenne Black Hills Stage Trail close to Stockade Beaver Creek where there is a tributary stream called Whoop-up Creek. The graders established their camp on the banks of that creek. It came to be known as Whoop-up Camp.

One of the only memorable things about the camp, besides the fact that it existed, was the demise of one man. His name has been forgotten, but his parting hasn't. One day, he was trying to get the cap off a 25-pound can of blasting powder. He wasn't having much luck, so he took a pickaxe, raised it over his head and slammed the point into the top of the can to make a hole in it. It made a hole all right. They could have buried the man in it if the explosion hadn't scattered him so badly.

Even though there was no burial, a monument was erected nevertheless. An old, broken scraper wheel was laid by the explosion site. An empty liquor bottle was placed in the hub. In lieu of flowers, tin tobacco tags were placed on the spokes.

Later the camp and its residents moved on, following the progress of the railroad. The memorial was the only thing left behind to mark the passing of these people.

The story bothers me. It makes me think of myself and my generation. I often wonder what tribute or memorial will be left to us—a rusted jet engine and a shorted computer chip, empty crack vials or bent hypodermic needles? Will people hundreds of years from now snicker and cluck at the foolishness of our own demise? Will that generation shake their heads saying, "They should have known better"?

The thing I think about the most, and that leaves me not with a sense of sorrow but with one of awe, is wondering what the future holds. What technology will come to pass that will overshadow and make obsolete the inventions we now enjoy and accept as everyday conveniences?

At that time, back in 1889, the building of the railroad was the ultimate industrial challenge. The graders moved across Wyoming building railbeds with their horse-drawn scrapers while in another place called Kitty Hawk, two brothers—Wilbur and Orville Wright—were repairing bicycles. As they worked, they dreamed of putting a flying machine into the air. Only fourteen years later, on December 17, 1903, Orville flew a 750-pound plane powered by a 12-horsepower engine. The 12-second flight carried him 120 feet. Later that day, Wilbur set a record by flying 852 feet in a 59-second flight. This was the day the jet age was born.

In less than one hundred years, planes have replaced trains. As I watch the space shuttle launches, I can see that the technology for people to live in space is not a science fiction dream but a reality. The next generation may come to take for granted weekend junkets to the moon, or vacations on Pluto.

I hope the future generation will remember that we lived in a world built on someone else's dreams. That on nothing but the strength of our own dreams, we built a foundation on which they can dream and build for their generations. Perhaps they will have the wisdom to know and appreciate this, and they will be able to build on the good things we have done and not repeat our foolish mistakes. ❧

Inheritance

When my grandfather died, his estate was made up of numerous bills, a few personal items and a large collection of books. As far as cash or material goods, he left nothing. But he did give me an inheritance that can never be measured in monetary or tangible ways. I have only recently come to appreciate the value of what he has given to me.

From the time I was a little girl, reading has been an important part of my life. My mother used to gather my four brothers, my sister and me around her each night to read to us. We fought over who got to sit next to Mom while she read out loud. I remember her reading *Old Yeller, Tom Sawyer, White Fang* and the biographies of Madame Curie and Winston Churchill. She was an excellent reader. I still get chills when I think about listening to her read *Call Of The Wild*. It was as if the people and characters she read about came to life and pulled us into their world.

Eventually I grew into adolescence and thought my friends were more important than being with my family. I thought spending the evening sitting on my mother's bed listening to her read was awfully childish. Luckily, I didn't get into that stage of my life before I had the pleasure of listening to her read *The Journals Of Lewis And Clark*. My brothers and sister and I loved the story. We became so fond of it, we started calling my mother's paperback copy of the book "Louie." One of us would always ask Mom, "Are we going to read some of Louie tonight?" Before she started to read, one of us would have to look under the bed and retrieve Louie.

We were almost finished reading it when my grandfather came for a visit. Grandpa, in his older age, had become very devoutly religious. My mother had recently divorced. This was one of Grandpa's "stop in and see how we're doing" checkup visits. He was sitting in the living room with my littlest brother, Eric, on his lap. My mother and I were setting the table in the adjoining dining room when we heard Eric's voice ring loud and clear. "Guess what, Grandpa?" he said, "Us kids got to go to bed with Momma and Louie last night."

Whoa! My grandfather came out of that chair and stood glaring at my mother with a white-faced, blue-lightning look. Did my mom talk fast. Two of us other kids had to stand witness to the truth of her story, and my sister showed him our copy of Louie.

I'm surprised Mom had trouble convincing him. She told me how grandpa used to gather her and her brothers and sisters on his bed to tell them stories. Only he didn't read. He made up his stories. For settings, he used the Wyoming mountains where he herded sheep. He would select three or four of the children and cast them as characters in the story he was telling. It was always preferable to be the hero. The hero wore nice clothes and rode the fastest horse. No one ever wanted to be cast as the villain. Grandpa gave the villain bad teeth or none at all. The villain couldn't see or hear, sometimes both. In the story, Grandpa mounted the villain on a broken-down or crippled horse and the trigger on his gun never worked at the most crucial moment. But worst of all, the villain drank coffee. The stories were so vivid that before Grandpa was finished, he had the child who had been selected to play the villain in tears and bawling.

Besides being a good storyteller, my grandfather loved books. As a child, he was forced to quit school after the fourth grade and went to work helping drive wagons. Later he herded sheep for a living. He eventually ranched and ran a sizeable herd of sheep in southern Wyoming. Even with his educational limitations and a life that demanded long days with hours of hard physical labor, there wasn't anything about the history of the world the man couldn't tell you. He taught himself to read by reading good books, but what he really loved was history, especially Wyoming history.

Grandpa owned so many books that he didn't have enough bookshelves for all of them. Except for the places where his bed and dresser stood, he had his books piled in neat stacks that reached from the floor halfway up around the four walls of his bedroom. Before his life ended, the room looked like it had a wainscot made of books. My grandfather died before I had a chance to realize the unspoken ways he influenced me.

Books have always been a part of my life, from the time I used to fight for a spot next to my mother to listen to her read. I think the way Mom chose the books she read to us had more to do with her being a busy mother of six who loved to read but couldn't find time for herself. Rather than selecting the books she read to us with any ulterior, literary or educational motives, Mom simply read to us from the books she wanted to read. Today she has more time and always has two or three paperback books scattered around her house. You can find them, spines pointing up, sprawled open, in her bathroom, bedroom, living room, kitchen and car.

I have tried to follow my mother's example. From the time Reuben and I adopted Min Dee, I have taken time each night to read to her. At first, Min Dee was small enough to fit in my lap, so we sat together in the rocking chair and read before bedtime. When she outgrew my lap, we moved to her room so we can snuggle in the pillows on her bed while we read before she goes to sleep. When we finish reading, I sing her a lullaby, tuck her in, get a fresh glass of water for her nightstand, give her a final kiss, then turn off the light and whisper, "Goodnight." It has become our reading-together ritual.

After I leave Min Dee's room, I usually go to my office to work on my writing. In my office, the bookshelves are completely full of books. I have other books piled in the empty floor spaces along the walls. Among all of these books, there is one very special book. It sits on a cabinet next to an antique typewriter. It is the size of an encyclopedia and weighs seven pounds. Along with a collection of family histories and historical articles written by various authors, the book also contains a complete and comprehensive history of Weston County, Wyoming. I am the author of that history. It is my first, published, book-length work. I deeply regret that my grandfather died before he could see it. He would have been so proud of me. The way he loved history, and storytelling, and the way he valued hard work, this book would have been a testament and tribute to him and all that he has given to me.

Sometimes I run my finger along the spine of the book and gently trace around the edges of the cover. When I do, I say a quiet prayer, not to God but to my grandfather, a sheepherder with a fourth-grade education. "Thank you, Grandpa. Thank you for making me so rich."

Aliens

One September day, I was driving home from town when I noticed our neighbor's pickup pulled off the dirt road and parked in the ditch. The driver's door was open, and our neighbor, Jim, was sitting on the edge of the seat with his legs hanging out the door. I stopped and rolled my window down. "Having trouble?" I asked. His response was a vacant stare. I knew something was wrong. Heart attack was the thought foremost in my mind. I quickly pulled my car off the road, jumped the gear shift into park and ran to the older man's side. "Jim, you okay?"

He shook his head and took off his beat-up felt hat. Sweat beads dotted his bald head. He hadn't shaved that morning, and grey and white whisker stubs poked out of his wrinkled neck. "It happened," he whispered.

"What happened?" I asked. The tone of his flat, quiet voice scared me.

He turned toward me but looked over the top of my head. "There's aliens in Russia."

"What?" I snickered. "Since when do you have to have a green card in Russia?" I wanted to laugh. Jim is a good rancher and a sharp businessman, but he's never above pulling a practical joke. I had the feeling I was being set up for a great punch line.

"I heard it myself. On the radio. Just a few minutes ago," he said seriously. "A spaceship landed in Russia. They have reporters there and everything. A bunch of scientists confirmed the report. I heard it right here on the radio. On the news."

I stared at him, unsure of what he had told me. But looking into his eyes, I knew this was no joke. The man believed and the power of his belief made me believe. I let myself slip down to sit on the running board next to his legs. "Really?" I whispered. "You know, I've always thought that, maybe, somewhere out there in a faraway place, there were others. But for them to be here, now?"

We couldn't look at each other. Instead, our eyes turned toward the sky. There is a vast difference between thinking something is possible and having to mentally accept that what you thought "was possible" is actually a reality. We sat for a long time not speaking. I tried to understand the ways this event was making me feel. I couldn't begin to comprehend the ways it would change my life and the world forever.

"They could blast us right out of the sky, if they wanted to," Jim finally said in a low, quiet voice. "They can probably blow up the whole planet."

After Jim spoke, I was able to give a name to what we both felt. Fear. We were sitting beside a dirt road in the middle of a Wyoming pasture, too scared to move or speak out loud.

The fear of being laser blasted out of existence by aliens from above filled him. But his fears were not my own. I had grown up with an atomic bomb mentality. As a child, I had come to know and even accept, on a certain level, the fact that within seconds and minutes we could be bombed into the next kingdom. Did it matter if the blast came from the other side of the earth or the other side of the universe? I had also grown up with the American superiority mentality. America is a nation that, for most of its history, has been superior in technological innovation, agricultural production and military strength.

These space invaders in Russia were obviously superior, even to America, in technology, military strength, and probably every other way. Accepting this fact made me feel very small.

We sat for awhile, then Jim started his pickup engine and tuned the radio to see if we could hear a news update. We found out that the alien story hit the broadcast wires prematurely. It turned out to be a Russian version of a *National Enquirer*-type UFO story. When the complete, original story was revealed, it contained a description of aliens that were thirteen feet tall and had three eyes. The spacemen were supposedly accompanied by a robot. A reputable source admitted that the three reported eyewitnesses were all children.

When we heard the explanation, Jim laughed and slapped his knee. "Boy, they really got one over on this old man, didn't they? It ain't even April Fool's day." He relaxed and laughed until his eyes watered. "What do you think of this old fool?" he asked me as he pulled a wrinkled handkerchief from his hip pocket and wiped his nose, eyes and brow.

"If you're an old fool, I'm a young fool," I told him. We joked about it for a few minutes, then talked about the weather before we climbed into our vehicles and went our separate ways.

We still tease each other about it. When I see him, Jim asks me, "Seen any spacemen lately?"

I tell him, "None I want to fly away with." We laugh, and others we have told the story to laugh. But when we laugh, for an instant, Jim and I look into each other's eyes and know that for a space of time, if only for a moment, we truly believed. And in that moment of belief, we were forced to recognize and acknowledge our fears.

I wonder about Jim. When he looks at the sky, can he do it without imagining some monstrous laser machine pointed at him? For me, the sky will never be the same. It used to be the visible and safe boundary of what I considered to be my world—it acted like the inside of an eggshell surrounding us, defining known reaches of knowledge, people and problems. But now, it lacks the protective substance of a shell. It is only a deep endless atmosphere in which the earth inhabits a minute part. I've always known this, logically and intellectually. But because of that day, that moment of believing there were really space aliens in Russia, I have come to accept this knowledge on another psychological and subconscious level. The universe is huge. We are not alone in it. When I look at the sky I don't fear laser blasters. Instead, I am afraid of being so small in such a big place. ✒

Min Dee's Hair

When we adopted Min Dee, the social workers gave us a photo album that contained a few pictures of her as a baby and a toddler. These were the pictures of Min Dee they had been able to collect for her adoption file. When she was born, her hair was copper red. At two years old, when we first saw her, it was a light reddish brown. Now, at eight years old, her hair has turned light brown streaked with blonde and red strands.

Min Dee was two years old when we brought her home to live with us. Her hair was short and so fine it felt more like down feathers than hair. When I tried to braid it, the strands slipped out of my fingers and wouldn't stay put. Min Dee, who was active and impatient, refused to sit still long enough for me to ever get it brushed to my satisfaction. I honestly thought that if I ever learned to braid her hair properly, I would be able to braid the fuzz on a tennis ball.

Min Dee insists on having her hair long. Over the years, I have kept the ends trimmed. As much as I seem to trim, it keeps growing. Now her hair reaches to her waist and she wants to brush and fix it herself. On the weekends, when we don't have to go anywhere, I let her take care of it herself. When I first allowed this, the results left her in tears. One time she ended up with more snarls than she started with. Another time it took us 30 minutes to untangle the brush that had gotten stuck in a ratty mess at the back of her head. Over time, she has learned how to handle the brush and coordinate her strokes so that she doesn't brush in more tangles than she brushes out.

I still insist on brushing her hair on weekdays. In the mornings, it is simply a matter of brushing it smooth, then pulling it into a ponytail or braid. At night, I take more time. I unwrap it from the elastic band and run my fingers through it to separate the strands. Starting at the bottom, I brush up into it until the brush slowly falls from the top of her head, down the length of her back to where the ends curl slightly at her waist. The red strands of hair reflect copper highlights and the blonde ones glisten and sparkle. Sometimes I lose myself in the hypnotic closeness I feel to her as I brush one stroke at a time.

When she has run out of patience, she interrupts, "Mom, are you done yet?"

I give one more quick stroke and put the brush aside. "There. All finished," I tell her.

The time is soon coming. I will brush her hair before bedtime, say, "All finished," and I will be. She won't sit still for me to brush her hair because she will want to do it herself while she talks on the telephone with her friends or boyfriends.

I've watched her. Lately, she has developed a way of looking out of the corner of her eye, sighing, then flipping her hair over her left shoulder. When she wants something from her dad, and he is stonewalling, first she turns on her eyes, gives a little audible sigh, then finishes with a coy, innocent-looking flick of the hair. Where her father is concerned, it's deadly. He usually gives in to her request. There have only been a handful of times it hasn't worked for her. I give her another six or seven years. By then, Min Dee will be using the same tactic, except she'll have finessed it by adding a slight, pouting quiver of the lower lip with a subtle, double combination flip-of-the-hips along with the hair. I doubt if she'll have any trouble getting a date for prom or anywhere else.

By then, she won't want me to fuss with or fix her hair. And I will feel too silly to ask—afraid that she won't understand how I long to take a brush, start at the ends, slowly work out the tangles, then watch the strands glisten and sparkle as I slowly pull the brush from the top of her head, down her back, to the ends of her hair. ✄

Stoneware

The summer before I married Reuben, I was working as a checkout girl in a grocery store. I saved every dime I could get my hands on, knowing that before long, I would need to set up housekeeping in my own home. One day I had gone into a gift shop to buy a card for a friend. While in there, I saw the most beautiful set of stoneware dishes I had ever seen. They were a light, creamy gold with a brown, country pattern called Village. I stood for a long time and looked at the set sitting on the display table. I picked up one of the plates and turned it over to look at the back. I held the cups and the saucers and ran my thumb over the pattern etched in the matching glasses. I had to have these dishes for my new home. Without any other thought than that, I wrote a check to put a set on layaway.

When I talked to Reuben on the phone that night, I couldn't wait to tell him about the dishes. After I did, his first question was, "How much did they cost?" When I told him they cost two hundred dollars, he came unscrewed. "Two hundred dollars?" he gasped, "Shelly? For dishes?"

"These are really special," I told him.

"Two hundred dollars worth of special? Shelly, they're just dishes. We can't do that kind of stuff with our money."

I don't remember the rest of the conversation, but it ended with me saying I would take the dishes back and get my deposit refunded. This was our first post-engagement, premarital disagreement. After I hung up the telephone and thought about it, I knew he was right. He was a $400-a-month ranch hand. It was careless and inconsiderate of me to spend two hundred dollars for something we definitely didn't need. The dishes would go back. They weren't worth fighting about, and they weren't worth the terrible way I felt, even if I really wanted them.

Later that night, the telephone rang at two a.m. It was Reuben. "I'm sorry," he whispered. "Please don't take them back. If you really want the dishes, I want you to have them. Please?"

"You were right," I answered. "We don't need them. Really."

"If you take them back, I'll be mad!" This remark led to our second post-engagement, premarital disagreement. Reuben finally told me, "Shell, I want you to have them, because if you marry me, it will be a long, long time before I can give you nice things, and I want you to have these, now."

We were married a few months later. I used the dishes that Thanksgiving, Christmas, and for Reuben's birthday the following February. I didn't have cupboard space to keep them in, so I stored them in their original packing cartons in the clothes closet of our spare bedroom. Each time I used the dishes, I refused to let anyone else wash them. I personally packed them back into their boxes before putting them away in the closet.

Later that spring, a neighbor lady, a woman in her forties, came to see me. I took out one of the plates to show her the pattern. She held it and said, "I had a set of stoneware once. Don't have any of it left. I lost some of the pieces every time we moved. I don't know how many just broke. But every single piece of it just chip, chip, chipped. All you had to do was look at the stuff and it chipped."

After she left, I put the plate into its carton. That day, when I set the box back into the closet, I put my stoneware dishes away for good. A couple of things made me decide not to use them anymore. It wasn't just the fear of breaking one of the pieces of the set—there was more to it than that. I had been out of the safety and security of living in my parents' home long enough to find out the harsh realities of life and living in the adult world. I had become perfectly well aware that everything—everything—is like stoneware. Whether it is promises, things emotional, physical, or spiritual, they can all be lost, broken and chip, chip, chipped.

I wouldn't allow my dishes to succumb to this fate. For a long time, even I didn't understand my actions or the reasons for refusing to use the dishes anymore. It drove Reuben crazy. When a holiday came around and I quietly set the table with my everyday dishes, he would say, "You spent two hundred dollars for a set of dishes you won't even use? That doesn't make sense, Shell."

I told him I knew it didn't make sense, but I was afraid of breaking one of the pieces. "So what?" he always asked with an exasperated shrug.

I didn't know how to verbalize my real feelings or thoughts. I was afraid he wouldn't understand or worse, that he would think I was silly.

One day, after we had been married for a few years, Reuben and I were in town taking care of some business. We had a little extra time so we wandered into a furniture store to look around. He saw a row of china hutches standing in the back of the store, tugged my sleeve and said, "Hey, look at this." We went and stood in front of a tall, dark-stained pine hutch. The polish of its smooth finish glowed in the showroom lights. "What do you think?" Reuben asked me. "Do you like it?"

"It's beautiful." I touched the smooth top and opened the upper doors with their lattice-framed windows. There were grooves cut into the back of the shelves to set plates up on their edges to show off their patterns through the windows.

"Do you like it?" Reuben insisted. I nodded. He turned and caught a salesman's eye. "I'd like to buy this for my wife," he said.

I frantically whispered, "Are you nuts? We can't afford something like this. Reuben. Reuben." I protested, but it didn't do any good. He was writing a check and giving the salesman directions to our house so the hutch could be delivered. I held my breath until we stepped out of the store. Standing on the sidewalk, I stopped, stared at him and said, "Reuben, we can't afford to do this with our money. Why did you do that?"

He put his arm around me. "We have the money in savings. I really want to do it. You bought that fancy set of dishes you won't use, only God and you know why. But if you aren't going to use them, I at least want you to show them off."

When the new hutch was delivered and set into place, I spent the better part of a day taking my dishes out of the boxes, carefully dusting them, and arranging them on the shelves. I stood the plates to the back and put the soup bowls and salt and pepper shakers in the front on one shelf. Then I set the glasses, cups and saucers on the second shelf.

Reuben thinks I never use these dishes. But he's wrong. I use them every day. When the world gets crazy and it seems like nothing stays together or fits, and the perfection they promise in heaven is too far away, all I have to do is look in the windows of my china hutch. For here is that little bit of tangible, visible perfection I need to make things feel ordered. Here are my stoneware dishes sitting in their places on the shelves, and not one piece is broken, lost or chipped. ✎

Priorities

Although it doesn't always appear so, I do like organization. When I decided to seriously try to see if I could be a writer, I gave a great deal of thought as to how I would fit it into my life. I sat down and did an evaluation of my responsibilities, interests and activities. I took everything I was doing, made a list and prioritized it. Watching television, social organizations and clubs were at the bottom. Those were the things I decided to sacrifice for what I hoped would turn into a career.

At the top of the list, I placed home and family in the number one spot. Next, at number two, came the ranch. I gave my writing third place. Having the order and importance of these things fixed in my mind has helped me immeasurably. It takes years and a tremendous amount of hard work and dedication to achieve anything in the publishing world. There have been times that I have been overwhelmed to tears by the frustrations and disappointments that go along with the writing business. I have found myself thinking, "Gee, it'd be great not to have any responsibilities except to write best-selling novels, one right after the other. If I didn't have to wash dishes, do laundry and take care of everybody, I'd be famous by now." And before I allowed these thoughts to go too far and turn into resentment, I made myself remember my priorities and what is most important.

After I had been writing for a few years and had received international recognition for my work, a turn of events helped me confirm the way I had set my original priorities. I hadn't felt well for the whole month of December. I forced myself to drag through Christmas which is my favorite holiday. I thought I had a flu bug or a cold. I couldn't breathe and felt tired all of the time. One day I walked down to the corrals. It was only forty or fifty yards, and I was used to being able to walk two or three miles without even thinking about it. When I got to the corrals, I was so out of breath I couldn't move. I leaned against the fence, closed my eyes and tried to calm myself. I knew something was wrong and stood there until I felt good enough to walk back to the house to call the doctor.

Two hours later, in his office, my doctor and I were looking at my x-rays. My chest cavity around my right lung was completely full of fluid. The cavity around my left lung was three fourths full. That night, in the emergency room of the hospital, the doctor gave me a lung tap. He inserted a hollow needle into my back between the ribs. When the needle was in place in my chest cavity, he used a large syringe to pull some of the fluid out. The doctors couldn't figure out what was wrong with me. They thought it might be a viral infection of some kind and decided to wait and see if I developed more symptoms. Two weeks later, I needed another lung tap. The fluid had come back. The second lung tap was followed by a third. I was getting worse, but they still couldn't figure out the cause of the problem. By the time I needed the fourth tap, I was on my way to a hospital in Denver.

After enduring every known medical test, trying out all of the fancy equipment, and seeing physicians from every department except pediatrics, the doctors in Denver decided the problem was my heart. The lining in the sac that surrounded it had become inflamed and was producing a fluid that was constricting my heartbeat. The constriction caused my blood to back up in my veins. The serum or fluid from the stalled blood was filtering out of my veins and settling in my chest cavity. The ultimate decision was heart surgery.

While I waited for the heart surgeon to come talk to me, the nurse told me I was extremely lucky because I was going to be operated on by one of the very best, that my surgeon was the same one who did the heart transplants for the hospital. The way she talked, I half expected him to arrive to the strains of organ music and a choir singing the "Hallelujah" chorus.

When he did come, he was accompanied by no less than a twelve-pack of other doctors, residents and interns. He whisked into the room, gave me a brisk handshake, introduced himself and in the same breath proceeded to describe what he was going to do to me. I'm not sure he was speaking in the same English language I know. I won't even attempt to reconstruct the medical terminology. What it boiled down to was, he wanted to open me up and cut a hole or "window," as he called it, in the sac that surrounded my heart. This would allow the fluid to drain away, the heart would be able to beat properly and consequently solve my problem.

When he finished describing the procedure, he went into the risks, hazards and side effects part of his discourse which began with this statement: "You could die if we don't perform the operation, but then you could die if we do perform the operation. There are possible risks and side effects." And he stated them one after the other until he came to the bottom line and said, without taking a breath, "Of course, there will be a scar, but that's a minor thing."

I looked that sucker right in the eye and said, "That's easy for you to say; you didn't buy a bikini at last year's end-of-the-season clearance sale." He stared at me, blinked, stared at me again, then lifted a teeny corner of his lip as he disappeared out the door. I turned to my family and said, "The man has no sense of humor."

Before the operation, it took four more lung taps to clear enough fluid out of my chest to make sure I would be able to breathe well enough to survive surgery. When it came time, I was ready. Ready to do anything to get it over with so I could go home and get on with my life. I felt confident; perhaps it was my body telling me that everything was going to be all right.

I tried my best to tell my family not to worry because I·was going to be okay. But when it came time to leave for the operating room, I knew I hadn't convinced them. My family was allowed to go most of the way downstairs to the operating room with me. I was moved from my bed onto a gurney and rolled into the elevator. The nurses, aides and my family crowded around me before the doors closed. They were all squeezed around me. I looked up at each of them. Min Dee stood quietly by my right arm, fascinated by all the machines, tubes and monitors that were connected to me. Her hand rested in mine. At the right foot of the bed was Reuben's sister, Kenda, wearing a brave smile, but I saw her turn away a couple of times to wipe her eyes. Next to her stood my mom, unable to hide her feelings of fear and torment. Her nose and eyes were red even though there were no tears. My stepdad was leaning against the wall of the elevator with his hand on my mom's shoulder. My father-in-law stood beside him clutching his cowboy hat while he tried to give me a comforting smile. Last, at my left shoulder stood Reuben holding onto my hand and arm.

I wanted to say something—crack some kind of joke that would make them feel better, or in some way assure them that everything was going to be all right. I couldn't say anything; I didn't dare. Each one of them had their emotions carefully balanced and had built mental safety zones to help them face the possible outcomes of what was about to happen. It would have been unfair of me to upset that. I had the easy part; in a matter of minutes, I would be asleep. They were going to be left with the hard part—waiting.

When I recovered, my family was gathered around the bed in my room with relieved and exhausted smiles. I felt bad for what they had been through and whispered, "I'm fine."

Over the next few days, the nurses and doctors began to pull the catheters, tubes, needles and monitors out of and off me. By the time I was well enough to go home we had been in Denver for a little more than two weeks.

When I was released, and we were driving home, Reuben wanted to stop and stay somewhere along the way so I could rest. He thought the 400-mile trip would be too much for me. I needed and wanted to be home. I had been gone far too long and made him drive until we got to our front door. After we arrived, I walked into each room so I could believe I was really home. That night as I fell asleep, my last thought was that I didn't think anything could possibly feel better than sleeping in my own bed.

After we had been home for two days, I felt restless and tired of being inside. When Reuben came to the house at noon for lunch, I told him I wanted to go out to feed the cows with him. He didn't think it was a good idea. I insisted. It had been such a long time since I felt the sun on my cheeks. The walls were closing in on me.

Reuben helped me climb into the four-wheel-drive pickup, and we drove to the pasture. I rolled down the window so I could feel the warm, March breeze on my face. Most of the snow had melted, leaving patches of green everywhere. Yellow buttercups bloomed along the edges of the remaining snow banks. Reuben turned the pickup off the road and drove across the sagebrush to a point where we could look out over the pasture and see the cows. When he stopped, the sage fragrance floated up, surrounding and filling the pickup cab. I started to cry. Reuben reached for me and asked if I tore my stitches. I shook my head, took a couple deep breaths, then sobbed. I was suddenly overwhelmed by everything; by what I had been through and survived, for being alive, for having a family that stands by me and having a home that smells like sage. No best-selling novel or success can ever replace these. Reuben wiped my face with his handkerchief and I whispered, "The sagebrush made me cry." ✺

Before
I Sleep

My grandmother could sleep anywhere. Anytime. One night, after dozing through a family dinner, she fell asleep in an easy chair in the living room. My brothers, sister and I were watching her. She would snore, scare herself half awake, mumble, then go back to sleep. We were snickering and counting the number of times she could snore in a minute. My mother caught us and sent us scattering with a deadly, evil-eye look.

I stopped in the doorway and watched Mom take an afghan and gently tuck it around Grandma's legs. She squeezed one of the wrinkled hands, then tiptoed away. It was a gesture of appreciation, a communication of affection from my mother to hers. I never fully understood it until I became a mother.

I fell into motherhood when my husband's teenaged sister, Kenda, came to live with us during her high school years. Every night, I thought my head would explode from the constant, thumping vibrations of the stereo in the room above mine. Whenever she went out at night, I would lie awake

69

needlessly worrying about car wrecks, drugs, booze and teenage sex.

I loved Kenda with all my heart and felt the proper amount of maternal guilt when I began counting the days before she, her boyfriend and her stereo would all go away to college, and I could sleep through the night again. Two weeks before she was to leave for the University, my husband and I adopted a little, two-year-old girl named Min Dee. We had been waiting for three years to adopt a child.

For a month after we brought Min Dee home, I got up three or four times during each night to check on her. Was she covered, too hot, too cold, breathing? She was always fine and sleeping peacefully. I decided she could make it through the night without my constant vigil. I needed some sleep. That night I settled into my bed with plans to stay there until morning but was shocked out of a deep slumber by a little person standing beside my bed. "Mom, drink water," Min Dee demanded.

I fumbled out of bed. After she took a mouse-sized sip from the glass, I tucked her into her bed and had barely gotten back to sleep when I felt something crawling over me. "Mom, scared. Sleep with you." She curled her body beside mine. I watched her sleep for a moment, then closed my eyes. Soon, I had a toe in my nose and an elbow in my stomach. I carried her back to her bed.

This became a nocturnal habit. With dark circles under my eyes, I asked my friend, a mother of three expecting four, "When do you get any sleep? When do you catch up?"

She laughed and said, "I haven't slept through the night since my first child was born nine years ago. If my kids aren't awake, I'm awake worrying about them. I have plans to catch up after they all leave home. Then I'll take mid-morning naps, noon naps, mid-nap naps, and afternoon snoozes. I figure I'll be caught up by the time I'm eighty-three years old."

Min Dee is now eight years old. She sleeps through most nights. But still, before I close my eyes at bedtime, I take mental inventory to make sure I have remembered everything she needs for school the next day: did we put the library books in her bag, she wanted to take a lunch instead of eat hot lunch, the spelling test is day after tomorrow. Many times, I find that I pull myself back out of bed or set the alarm for the dark hours of morning to do something for her. Perhaps the favorite pair of jeans she asked to wear aren't washed, maybe I need to bake cookies for milk-and-story hour at school. There never seem to be enough hours for all of the needs. I always worry that I will neglect some little thing that makes a big difference to a child.

I've found that you never stop worrying. I still worry about Kenda even though she has grown into a beautiful woman and is settled into adulthood. She broke up with her high school sweetheart, finished college and has married a man who loves her with all of his heart. Her stereo has a place of honor in the living room of her new home. Recently, she gave birth to her first child. They named the baby, a little girl, Katelyn and call her Katie.

On their first visit to our house after Katie was born, Min Dee and I squeezed into the rocking chair so that, together, we could hold and rock the baby. Kenda had dark circles under her eyes. She sprawled on the couch and said, "I'll be so glad when she starts to sleep through the night. I feel like I haven't slept in a hundred years."

A joyous snicker rose inside my heart. I cuddled the baby close and whispered, "Katie, are you keeping your momma awake?"

My grandmother had nine children. It's no wonder she slept through supper. My mother had six children and probably needs to sleep through supper. And me? I have a while to go before I sleep. Quite a while.

For now, I cherish the times when Min Dee kept me awake with her toes in my ears and her knees in my ribs, and I was forced to carry her back to her bed. I will remember those brief moments she huddled in my arms before she fell asleep, then squirmed from my grasp. I know that soon, too soon, she will be out dancing under a crepe-paper canopy at a high school dance. She will have boyfriends who, in some lovely, romantic, starlit place, will promise their undying love forever-more. And I will be at home. Awake. Only this time, while I'm awake and waiting and worrying, I won't be in bed. I'll be sitting up, making use of the time. I'm going to learn to crochet. I have plans for an afghan. It will be made of the finest yarn I can buy in a light, muted shade of pink, my mother's favorite color. ✿

Cracker
Soup

Somewhere in my childhood, I acquired a self-esteem problem. I grew up feeling unworthy, that I had never been and never would be good enough. I used to spend hours trying to evaluate and reevaluate my life in order to trace the roots of my character. I had grown up in a close, loving and supportive family. I had no reason to feel the way I did. When I tried to figure out my problems, instead of finding answers, mostly I just gave myself a big headache of confusion. I wasted my early childhood wondering who I was. My junior high school years were spent trying to cope with pimples and hormones. In high school, I struggled with a weight problem. At five foot three, 150 pounds, I had my hands full. By the time I went to college, I had shed most of the extra weight but was back to wondering who I was and why I felt like I was a terrible person. Worse, those questions were compounded by another dilemma. I had to decide what I was going to do with the rest of my life.

Love solved the latter problem. I fell in love, married Reuben, and we set out to conquer the world with three assets: an old car, a blue heeler puppy named Idget and a dream. Someday, we were going to own a ranch of our own.

I had found something good and satisfying to do with my life, but the old self-esteem problems continued to haunt me. I imagined that I wasn't a good wife, that I wasn't a good enough housekeeper, that whatever I did, it would never be good enough. I was on the verge of becoming a neurotic perfectionist.

I overcompensated, always trying to do better. Sometimes, I swept and dusted the house twice a day. I did everything that I thought was expected of wives, only double. It still wasn't good enough.

By the time Reuben and I had been married a few years we experienced a lot of changes. We purchased his father's ranch, traded off our old car for a newer old car and Idget had given birth to several litters of puppies. In all that time, my feelings about myself didn't change. I hadn't been able to overcome them and probably would have ended up in a padded cell if it hadn't been for Reuben's older sister, Emma Jean.

One night when she was visiting, we were sitting around the table after supper. She and Reuben were reminiscing about their childhood experiences. The topic of conversation turned to food and the way their mother made them eat the things they didn't like. Emma Jean laughed and said, "Do you remember having cracker soup?"

Reuben answered, "It wasn't so bad. Better than going to bed hungry."

I had lost the thread of the conversation. "Hold on, you guys," I interrupted. "Cracker soup? I've never heard of it."

Emma Jean explained that when they were kids, if their mother was too tired to cook, she fixed cracker soup for them. The kids crunched soda crackers into cereal bowls while their mother put the teakettle on the stove. When it whistled, she poured the hot water over the crackers and added a little butter. This was cracker soup. My mouth fell open. "Cracker soup?" I gagged. "I can't stand soggy crackers. It sounds terrible."

Emma Jean giggled. "It wasn't too great. I always swore I'd never give it to my kids. But you know what? Now that I am a mother, there are days I just get to the end of my rope and I'm so worn out, I find myself putting the kettle on the stove and grabbing the crackers. It's a last resort. But sometimes, I think I'll go nuts if I don't give myself a break."

Those words hit home. A person has to have a break now and then. For the first time in my life, I realized I had never, ever given myself a break.

For Reuben's mom, cracker soup served its purpose. She lived a two-hour drive away from a fast food hamburger chain or bucket chicken joint. Home pizza delivery is simply unheard of out here on a ranch. For her, cracker soup was a save-my-sanity fast food. For Emma Jean, cracker soup is her "I've had it, I need a break meal." Since I heard about it, I've used cracker soup, too, but not in the same way. Instead, I use it as a touchstone.

I am acquainted with a historian named Watson Parker. He wrote a book about the history of gold mining in the Black Hills of South Dakota. He told me where the term "touchstone" came from. In olden days, a black silicious schist rock called a touchstone was used to test the purity or goodness of a sample of gold. The gold to be tested was rubbed or "touched" against the rock. The gold made a mark or streak on the touchstone, and its quality or purity could be judged by the color of the mark it left in the rock.

I finally gave myself a break and took time to realize that what was wrong with me was that my mental touchstones were unrealistic. I had spent my life measuring or testing my self-worth against standards of perfection no one can possibly live up to. I had never established my own touchstones or comfortable standards for doing things. I took time to look at myself and decided that I like me, faults and all. Then I told myself that as long as I never, ever, serve cracker soup, I don't have to work until I drop, and it won't change the fact that I am still a good and valuable person.

It wasn't an overnight change and took several years to gain confidence in the idea of using my cracker soup touchstone. But it worked.

Now there are times, not always, but times I think my house can qualify for a federal disaster loan to help with the cleanup. There are weekends my laundry room is nothing but a giant, bottomless, dirty clothes hamper. I've been a couple of months behind in the bookkeeping and six months behind in the filing. There are moments I seem so disorganized, I can't find the pen I'm holding in my right hand. That's when those old self-defeating, self-deprecating feelings creep over me and press into my conscious thoughts. But I fight them back by taking a few seconds to give myself a break. When I do, I pause a minute to think about it, take a deep breath, plant my feet squarely under me, place my hands firmly on my hips and say out loud, "Yes, the house is a wreck, my life is a disorganized mess and I'm not sure what my own name is. But as bad as things are, it's okay, I'm still a good person. After all, I have never, ever, served cracker soup."

Homemade Bread

My grandmother used to bake 25 loaves of bread a week. She and my grandfather were ranchers with a crew of four or five ranch hands. When I was young I worked for them in the summertime. My job was to help Grandma.

Every Monday morning, after I finished washing the breakfast dishes, Grandma would tell me to get the bread pan. It was a five or more gallon, enamel wash basin, the kind you might see hanging on the side of a sheep wagon. Grandma's bread pan hung from a nail on the back wall of the pantry.

Within minutes of handing the pan to her, she had milk, lard, yeast and flour poured into it and was elbow deep in sticky bread dough. As she mixed and pushed at the mass, her grey bangs wilted down over her eyes. Her breathing came harder and heavier as the dough thickened into a solid ball. My job was to stand beside her with a tin sifter full of flour. Each time she nodded, I shook more flour around the edges of the pan so she could work it into the dough.

Sometimes I couldn't help myself. I'd reach out and try to snitch a piece of dough to eat. I hoped she wouldn't notice, but I always got caught. Without looking up or breaking her concentration, she would order, "Don't fuss in the food. You know I don't like fussing in the food." And I would pull my hand away, place it back on the sifter and try to look contrite and obediently dutiful.

When she was done mixing and kneading, the bread dough rose while we made the beds, shook the rugs, and swept the wooden floors. Then Grandma shaped the loaves and placed them into greased pans that I handed to her as she needed them. When the pans of swelling dough lumps filled her small counter, we covered them with white tea towels and let them rise again while I washed all of the bread-making dishes. By the time I was done, Grandma was pulling the last batch of golden loaves from the oven and dumping them out of the pans onto the counter. It was a moment of triumph, a moment of having a large and essential task completed.

When the last loaf had been dumped out, Grandma would throw her hot pads into the only remaining space left in the corner of the counter. Wiping the bangs from her face with her forearm and then carefully, so not to burn her fingers, she would break the last loaf of bread open and let the steam flow from it. Then she gingerly tore it into five or six pieces. Taking one of the pieces in her fingertips, she slathered it with butter, sprinkled it with a spoonful of sugar, then turned, bent over slightly and placed it into my cupped hands. After a very brief smile, she turned back to the cupboard and began pulling things out of the shelves for making lunch.

I never, ever, remember a time my grandmother actually and verbally said, "Shelly, I love you." From the time she woke in the mornings until she dropped into bed at night, she worked too hard to be philosophical, emotional, or sentimental. She never gave words: she didn't have to. Instead, we shared the task of baking bread. It's been many years since she passed away. But still, I can't walk into a bakery, pass the bakery counter at the grocery store, or smell bread baking in my own oven without thinking about her and feeling her standing next to me ready to nod for more flour. ❧

Magic Mike

I swore I would never be one of those mothers who turn into driven, red-eyed monsters at Christmas time. I saw fifty of them in a department store a few years ago. They were clawing and tearing at each other over a shipment of twelve Cabbage Patch dolls. After the poor salesman brought them out of the back room, he barely escaped with his life.

I never understood what turned sweet, domesticated women into raving fanatics until the year Min Dee was five years old. I had taken her to the mall to see Santa two days before Christmas. For more than a month before that, I had been asking her what she wanted Santa to bring her. I always got one of two answers—I don't know, or everything in the toy section of the Sears Christmas catalog.

When Min Dee's turn came to visit with Santa, she crawled up onto his lap and told him, "I want one thing and one thing only—a robot."

I spent the rest of the day trying to think of a good, Christmas morning explanation as to why Santa brought doll furniture instead of a robot. How do you explain to a five-year-old that one of the harsh realities of life is that you don't always get what you want?

I couldn't do it.

Early the next morning, I set out on a dragnet search that covered a 130-mile radius. By late afternoon, my nerves were frazzled, my eyes bloodshot. I was sick to death of unsympathetic sales people telling me, "I'm sorry, we're all out of robots. They have been such a popular item this year. If we had known, we would have ordered more."

I finally found myself in a fancy electronics store. "Do you have robots?" I begged.

"We have one model left. Come this way," said a tall, blonde, curly-headed salesman with a big, let-me-help-you smile. He showed me a two-foot-tall, metal, monster-looking, electronic marvel. "This robot," the salesman exclaimed, "can be programmed to serve drinks at your cocktail parties, answer the door and take out the trash. And it comes with battery recharge cable, all for only four hundred and fifty dollars."

"Four hundred and fifty dollars? Four hundred and fifty dollars?" I screeched as I grabbed him by the tie and jerked him down so I could look at him eyeball to eyeball. "ARE YOU CRAZY? At my parties we pass the bottle. As for answering the door and taking out the trash, what do you think I wanted kids for in the first place?" The salesman turned a little blue around the lips. I let go of his tie and left in tears.

I tried, I really tried. There wasn't a robot to be had anywhere. I looked around. A block down the other side of the street, I saw a little mom-and-pop hardware store. "One more time," I thought as I took a deep breath.

And that is where I found Magic Mike, the talking, walking robot. There were only three left on the shelf. I grabbed one and cradled it in my arms. Magic Mike is fifteen inches of silver and red plastic on wheels. He can't answer the door or take out the trash. He doesn't really talk. But, in a silicon-chip voice, he can say, "Hello. I am the atomic-powered robot." He doesn't actually walk. He just rolls around and bumps into things while he pops, squeals, squawks, buzzes, beeps and in general, makes more noise than twelve little girls at an ice cream party.

But for Min Dee, the child who wanted him and saw him under the tree Christmas morning, he was pure magic.

That's when I realized, there's plenty of time to learn about the harsh realities of life. For as long as I can, I will kick, bite, scratch and claw my way across towns and cities to get whatever little thing Min Dee might want for Christmas. Because I know, that for the short time she is a little girl, Christmas is my one chance to create magic, the magic of giving something wanted and hoped for, the magic of making a wish or dream come true, the magic of Christmas. 🎄

Christmas Cookies

I can't imagine life without laughter. It would be like Christmas without homemade cookies. Around our house, everyone has his or her preferred choice when it comes to Christmas cookies.

Reuben believes that you might as well not have Christmas if you don't have springerles (pronounced spring-las). They are rock-hard, German cookies flavored with anise seeds. It takes two days to make them. The dough, mostly made of sugar and eggs, is mixed, kneaded for thirty minutes, then rolled and cut into circles. Designs are pressed into them with a clay cookie stamp. The cookies then sit overnight on baking sheets sprinkled with more anise seeds and are baked the next day. The warm, heavy licorice aroma from the oven fills the house and lasts for a week. After cooling, the springerles are placed in a tin to mellow. At the end of two weeks, they're so hard they have to be dunked before they can be eaten. It's not unusual to soak up a half a cup of coffee before you can take a bite out of one.

Min Dee's favorite is sugar cookies cut into Santas, stars, bells and angels. She likes them for no other reason than they offer the greatest opportunity to play in the dough and "help Mom." What makes them unique is a secret hint my grandmother gave to me. Add a teaspoon of grated lemon peel and a pinch of mace to the dough for an unusual flavor.

My favorite Christmas cookie is chocolate crackles. The fudgie dough, made richer with a teaspoon of cinnamon and a hint of ginger, is shaped into little balls and rolled in powdered sugar before baking.

There are other kinds of cookies that I bake for the holidays. Almost all of them are family recipes that have become traditional Christmas fare. Each has its own blend of spices and ingredients like nutmeg, molasses, allspice, ground cloves and ginger.

It's funny—cookies are not my favorite thing to bake. By the time they are mixed, rolled, cut and baked in endless batches one after another, they're a lot of work. Heaven knows, none of us need to eat that many cookies. But it just wouldn't be Christmas without a house and kitchen filled with the smell of cookie spices. That's what makes the cookies special— the spices. It's the same with humor and my friends and my family. Our love and shared laughter is what adds the flavor, the aroma, and the richness to life. They are the spice. ✺